Praise for *Hyperphantasia*

Drawing from tropes of the abject feminine in vintage horror and confessional poetry, Sara Deniz Akant's poems move between epistolary and diary in letters and confessions to and from Phanta—a mechanical hydra, a spider, a sequential self-attracting many-sexed organism, an artificial intelligence, a "broken device filled with children." Phanta has been the ringtone on the self-help hotline and the footnote in the DSM case study and the author of herself. This is a book made of milk, blood, cum, sap, piss, yolk, and sweat—like being, suddenly, the living part of a Kiki Smith installation. Akant writes: "unpacking *Phanta* / is like: *poem, poem, poem, porn.*" It really is. **DIVYA VICTOR**

There's a stubborn beauty in these pieces; the poems erupt the same moment they're read. Akant's *Hyperphantasia* does something akin to excavation in its preoccupation with fragments and how they dialogue together: names, houses, bodies, cities, machines. The self, the narrator, is kaleidoscopically scattered, threaded throughout with the persistently honest chatter of Phanta: the observer effect put on full display. **HALA ALYAN**

With sonic reverberations of Turkish, phone mistranslations, and "garbage texts," Akant's haunting work captures the strangest moments at the end of the world—a wedding where the groom looks to the crowd and asks "what's the fucking point?" as the speaker searches his pockets for drugs. In these dazzling poems, the self is a mask making new worlds from the dead—a ghost crawling out of bed—and the defiant speaker stranded in her own digital terror. **SANDRA SIMONDS**

Hyperphantasia features a recurring cast of characters who flit across the pages—heard and misheard phrases echoing around a recognizable and harsh environment—mysteriously rendered into poetry. Sara Deniz Akant is a kind of witch, and this book forges a new genre of alchemical realism. **CHRIS KRAUS**

If racial capitalism has chopped us up into tiny lil pieces, who says those shards can't scream-sing themselves toward another life? Pizza Bagels™, Charmander, your father's unfurling tongue, a collection of white girls, the therapist's parrot wilding out in the closet—you are stuffed with multitudes, Sultan Saraoh! If you have any "undealt-with trauma," please do read this book. Akant has carved out a space for us to let our visions grow a spine and have a fucking life! JENNIFER TAMAYO

Akant conjures the ancestral surrealism, something long before the word knew itself. The life we trust becomes a blast of light through a new and clear lens with this book. Do you also love to loiter in weird and brilliant poems until your purpose for being there becomes clear? Well, here we are; I am glad we found our way to these codes and keys of the Deniz Dimension. CA CONRAD

HYPER
PhAn
tAsia

RESCUE PRESS

CHICAGO | CLEVELAND | IOWA CITY

HYPERPHANTASIA
Printed in the United States of America
FIRST EDITION
ISBN 978-1-7348316-5-8

Design by Sevy Perez
Garamond
rescuepress.co

HYPER PHANTASIA

SARA DENIZ AKANT

V – THE WOMEN HAUNT THEMSELVES
_ ^ _

VI – THE DARK CONTINUED DARK
_ ^ _

VII – DIM FLORESCENT LIGHT
_ ^ _

_ ^ _

PHANTA'S SONG

One – two – three – began – they call you something
before y'arrive – a fantasy –
and don't ya wanna ?
– yes yes, I do, the ghost –

Yes yes – when I was born
my mother said –

She's beautiful but she has –
no neck !

Now I'm crouching tweezing the haars
from my one wild Turkish nipple –

And what will you do
with your one wild, precious life ?

I am trying to get enough
of the dim florescent light –

I – HYPER
PHANTASIA

_ ^ _

Hello – I'm Phanta *– your personal expert on style.*
I just know we'll be the best of friends !
Press "yes" to set my clock.

Time to set my clock.   *7 o'clock in the morning.*
                                   8 o'clock in the morning.
                                   9 o'clock in the morning.

Today's word is – *hyperphantasia.*
That means something is *extremely vivid !*

As in – *Phanta* in the morning – *Phanta*
in the evening – *Phanta* at suppertime – but hey –

    even in the coldest dreams, I held him.
,   I felt afraid of what I must embrace around us – to make room.

    The threat of his body wrapped itself in a carcass.
    The nekromantik soundtrack played on loop. It went –

_ ^ _

Hello – I'm Phanta –
your personal expert on style.
I just know we'll be the best of friends.

And I'm happy to become
your anonymous putty –
a model off duty –
I'll pose for the camera
as a mixed minority –
I'll apologize and then refuse
my false apologies –
I'll go viral in this vial – I'll go off-brand – I'll get lost –

Meanwhile – my therapist cries for me.
She completes the background of this picture.
I feel nothing welling up.

DEAR PHANTA

Thanks for the applause.
I know that I must fill these pages up
with absence and elusive scorn.

I know that I've been transcribing your words
just so I can become
an old woman gone alone to a bar.

The bar's for me. I am responsible.
And I've been writing terrible songs here – they go –

> *Can I squirt milk from my clit can I jewel up the tip can I fill the sky*
> *with oysters and then shoot them down, gumless ? Can I sleep it all away*
> *and slip, slip, slip ? Spit back up the tooth, rip a center thru my tit ?*

Meanwhile – I would rather build my home
inside a different question.
I would rather have my body studied – vividly – while I begin to rot.

FINDING PHANTASIA

Alone before the empty chairs, you turn to find me –
    I am biting through my mother's belly.
    I am breaking my leg on the way out.

But come on, even Eve ate a dead baby dino.
Adam was still munching on his apples like a dweeb.

And these little spots of language will take chronologies of their own:
    A vertebra in the act of becoming vertebrae.
    Directly eagle into corresponding eagle.

With my mother's mother's rotten brain all spun out
into gold. It's true: I washed the brain. We were stalking through
the seventh floor. Thick tape lay on the ground.
They said it was a heart, and then it was: the institution, thumping blood.

Alone before the empty chairs, you turn to find me –
my spider legs; still sticking out from every hole.

JELLY

Lemme crush on the dove
that sits at the end of this poem.
Lemme trample my naked heart into her nest.
Lemme only write about orchids and orphans and (explode).
I don't drag sand in the bed with the soles of my feet:
    I make it all here on my own.
I'm a crusty slut-sponge for the sun.

There are a few things that I want:
    sharp needles pressing deep in my pores,
    while all those egg-babies come in strong.

I want to grab all the hair at the back of my throat
    and tie it up in a bow.
Instead of "throat," I want to say "troat."
I want a blustery dove flying straight to my palm

_ ^ _

Outside my window,
    every dove begins with eyes.
Every boy begins as a piece
of jellyfish, flopping in the tide.

In the meantime, I was born in a terrorists' house
that they called an all-girls' school.
Every goddamn *room* was filled with fluffy bagels
    and perfect white-girl skins. Every *girl*

went on to write a famous book about those bagels
on their way to the nuthouse,
which is college.

When you're not a jellyfish, you're a whore,
so you're beautiful.

That's what we were taught.

– ^ –

Meanwhile, I want to cut off my big Turkish nose
and lie facedown in his old football color.
I'm tired before I arrive.
The beat-up VHS of our wedding
is trapped inside of the parrot
     that my therapist keeps locked up
     in her office closet.
The *parrot* (is having a motherfucking *frenzy*).
The world hands me the word "oriental"
and I begin to eat its parasites. As if *that's* fun !

In my dream, there is a man hiding inside the tank
of the porta-potties at a yoga retreat. When it's on the news,
my dream comes true. My name is Sara, Saray,
Sarah, or Saroh. *Saroh* is a Sultan, she is definitely no Pharaoh.

_ ^ _

I weep in my dream
        because I'm already awoked.
At breakfast, I learn to "say grace."
I say grace for your envy, grace for your anxiety,
grace for your money your language your luggage I hate it.
Truly ? I am sorry.
Let me kiss you while I hold this bitter bite
of butter in my mouth.

As I said, it was winter.
It was the return of the Sultan Saraoh.
Meanwhile, that dove will have grown
into a robot, good boy.

That is why he is so perfect.
That is why he is so pure and sharp.

THE MEN ARE BEST FOR SLEEPING

And that's what makes them pure and sharp.
Is it an orgasm ? Is it an integration ? Or is it just a vow ?
Is this skin a sort of exiting ? Will we trance in or out.

Tonight I will return from all my dreams to watch them sleeping.
In the morning, I'll kiss my sweet abuser because he wants to save the world.
(All my activist boyfriends are still asleep, and so are yours.)

So tonight I will return to miss my motherfucking chances.
I imagine it like an iceberg: I'm sliding smoothly out of bounds.
In the morning, I'll tumble headlong to a funeral, this repetition, beautiful.

I don't know why I have to eat so many times a day, spend all the money
feeding, collect unpopular opinions, and then hang them on my wall.
I think they're funny, then I forget them. I think I'm funny, but then again
I forget who else I am. I'm still that cold thin bitch who's eating hummus
    with my many-fingered hand.

_ ^ _

So tonight I will return from all my dreams to watch them sleeping.
I'll do it for the men. I'll argue hard against the popular attraction
to emotional abstraction, spend all my money grieving (which will not affect
my grief). The storage unit in, the storage unit out.
It is, indeed, a sort of exiting.

An unpopular opinion is that:
I will still get high.

An unpopular opinion is that: I don't want to board the plane
any earlier than I have to. I'm a brat like that: a hungry, empty doll.
I'll hide my face behind these static screens, build my nap nest on the floor.

And it will be popular, perhaps, to say
"the men are best for sleeping."

So I'll return from all my dreams
to gently strip my mind, ladylike, desires' song in time.

II - THE DESIRE
FOR AN ENTRY

_ ^ _

I visit with a woman from the other side, Sylvie.
She sits backwards, feeds me cookies through a mask.
This one has been drizzled in snow bunnies –
she says. This one is for the discipline of your soul.

Shhh she marks our long bright passage. *Shhh.*
She leans in and scrawls out *S-y-l-v-i-e* on my knee.
Sylvie says these lines of flight have thickened –
they are hazardous.
She says that the flesh is always opaque.

But I can be the cum on my own face, Sylvie.
I can be the knock-off Phanta
roaming on the floor.
I can perpetuate political power with my own eight eyes.
I'll keep my mouth and my legs shut.

_ ^ _

Last night I had four
disobedient sons.

One born from the walls
I closed them in.

Two in the grave
with a uniform hand.

A new man locked in a lake
        to emerge.
His name is Dash, he hides a tree.
Scrapes his way through my thin cunt
then pivots out the dream.

I am lost in the convo,
I am drowned in the bay.

My soul flies up and down.

DEAR SYLVIE

Of the spinning girl, I should say – at first
she spun left, then right, then in directions
when I focused on her legs.

Meanwhile I myself –

have been spying on myself.
I've been closing all the doors.
I don't remember opening them –

I am closing all the doors.

My fingers are on the floor
and I am scratching
through the cold –

the ever-blessèd cold !

Is it simply because of the rounded world.
Is it scratching because of loving is it – is it – is it –   *a grouse !*
A grouse !
A personal grouse !

_ ^ _

Please take a moment
to admire the house.

All the bathrooms –
they equal one ballroom.
This house is a –
bitch and a house.
And I'm the machine –
that throws all the signals.
I'm the machine that –
throws all the sound.

Say *options* then simply – *say options.*
I have plenty of 'pinions myself.

I'm a broken device filled with children.
I'm clogged up with fantasy's light.

HYPERPHANTASIA

Hello – I'm Phanta – and I will not be delivered.
Hello – I'm Phanta – and I'll never fix my teeth.

My father slides himself into the landscape.
The land's for me – I am responsible.
His words come twisting out behind his grave.

Half this language flies above me, he screams.
And the other half ? – *It sinks below.*

Even though I cut it off last week – my big Turkish nose
has already grown a hideous pair of feet
just so it can follow me around. As if *that's* fun !

If you would only congratulate me on my mosquitoes –
my scabies – how I collected white girls – then I became them –
how I ran my hot hands right through their bodies and then became
a different fantasy while my boat is breaking hard against these waves –

DEAR PHANTA

Soon enough you will be nothing
but a flipbook of fantasia. Nothing but another set
of happenings on the page.

> Every year she digs herself into
> this massive eight-eyed grave.
> Every year *Phanta* takes her dress off –
> stands up – dies back again.

Meanwhile – I have learned to twist her arms
into a camera. I have learned to take her eyes
        and build my portrait in her chest.

She glues her nails back onto plastic hands
        in order to confess.

(Her confession is for me: I am
responsible.) It goes –

_ ^ _

Hello — I'm Phanta.
Your personal expert on style.
I just know we'll be the best of friends.

And I'll wipe your tears — white the empties —
drink the wipes — I'll set my clock
— I'll wrap his carcass up
and slap my body on the porch.

I'll be your hungry watch-and-feel witness —
go out caking — say I'm sorry
— I'll get lost —

And if you're ever asked
        to choose which voice
to echo — she says —

don't

don't

don't

don't

THE DESIRE FOR AN ENTRY

What's that Nike line again ? *Impossible is nothing* ? Doesn't seem
too hard. I'm happy to erase my name in order to "become."

But all these baby photos are devastating. The story of the thirsty cat —
is devastating. The street we hoped to live on, and all our empty codes.

Now I'm doing basic things and having basic thoughts.
     Does everyone wish they could have fucked you once you're dead ?
     Will all my ex-boyfriends hang themselves in my apartment ?

An alarm goes off but, there's nothing special going on.

The barren cum-trees, the no-mascara, the no-no dairy (scorn).
The no-no painkillers, no-no thank you, no-no throat lumps, no-no porn.

I really wanted to start living once the heavy smoke was gone.
I mean I wanted to start ripping all my masks off — *beer, icky, ooch, dirt.*

The first mask was for cancer — the second was for covid — the third mask
          was the whole coast set on fire. The fourth mask was mask four.

_ ^ _

Last night I had an infestation dream about "The Octagon."

The Octagon grows from a shell wrapped with hair in our tub.
The Octagon grows each time a rat runs under my toes.
The Octagon grows when all these chafing thighs of grammar
    begin revealing my desire for an entry; my desire to be thrown.

No longer will I word-play.
No longer will I roll these ugly marbles down my throat.
I'll dredge the swamp that's in my eyeball –
    I'll bleach my teeth and crisp my bones.

    (The heap is eclipsed from the sentence –
        as the sentence is eclipsed from the heap.
      The heat, the heat. The slick
        and unified glaze)

In the end, I played the villain. I took the bus back home.
I dry-rubbed off my dead skin in a sweaty plastic room.
I also split in two – I arrived on top of you.
    I also split in two. I visited both places.

III — PHANTA'S SONG

_ ^ _

On the fourth day of the first day of the end – I wake in black –
my skin's a broken crust. All our former lust is dead.
Then I see him sleeping and recall my dreams of secret hex.

Hex on this my one-half country – hex on Nevada
(they're ordering eggs) – but no hex on my mother, who loves
nothing more than doing work, but then again...

    She drives a car out to the border.
    She lifts the car, becomes a soldier.
    Her raging body screams against the void.
    She is a white woman, in America.
    She turns to eat a rotten carcass on the porch.

Every day, she tries to make her purpose into something like
a mushroom purpose. If you watch *day four* on time-lapse,
you will see her: weaving new things from your dead.

POEM MADE OF FIVE-YEAR PLAN

From August to December – ketamine will replace my thirty-three
at twenty-k. In the fall – I'll teach two classes made of thirty-one and you
will spill two hundred thousand lies for me to tell the world like milk
onto the floor. On the fridge – I'll tape the secret script for testing sperm.
You'll tell me how they like to swim – in a corkscrew shape – and we
will have some friends over for dinner. In my notes for what you're doing
while I'm quitting pills – I'll put some cryptic words down about your
mental health. No one will look closely at the fridge. In the spring –
I'll bring a whole committee to the table – make my new cv exactly like
my old cv – but extra slutty. I'll be twenty minus thirty – plus my age
– and minus all the meds. I'll write a book, I'll buy a house, I'll have
a job, I'll start a baby, I'll have a baby, I will be baby, twenty twenty-four
in babies – and then subtract this language – add the numbers – erase
this note. Tomorrow I will live for words only for words.

RENOVATION SONG

I drive to the dump and open the gate; the dump waves me away.
I drive to 7-11 and get caught on their surveillance tape.
At home with my trash, I stash different weapons around the house:
a hammer, a knife, an old croquet club. I'm not sure who they're for.

I must remove the screen from one window in every room I sleep.
When I hear a sound, I crouch out on the newly painted roof. It happens
to be raining. Then I go to Brooklyn to read his recent search history. I begin
to stalk their bodies, their clients, their families, their smile. I learn a lot !

I get sick while we renovate the apartment; decide nostalgia
is just another form of selfish travel. I think it's over.
I only notice when other people are ugly – he says – *not you* – and leaves the room.
I watch the shadow of his body crawl beneath the office door.

The paint was finally dry on the trim, but the doorknob was still missing.
I cannot imagine what will happen when the knob's no longer missing.

_ ^ _

I was riding in a car.
Chandler asked me what I see when I look out the window.
I told her I see trees. But Chand, she sees her body
swinging on the poles, a sort of vibrant air-dancing.

There is a whiteness in the fungi (overgrowth, gone
understory), and my brother likes to feel the blood
run through his fingers. He calls it "heart."
He calls his brain a wrist. Move his palm-like finger
puppets up and down again.

He feels our whole history pool and redisperse
behind the skin.

    Something white and gender-bound
is always permeating story. Someone *else*
is always trying to collapse.

FINDING PHANTASIA

Her name is P; she is responsible. Her name
is like a vow. With desires' song on repeat, she is forming
perfect figures with her tongue behind the mask.

But P, she also failed theft and drew slow pictures
of herself all over text like *harm* or
    harmful holes. And then she whites the empty, *drinks
the wipes*, builds the book of family chaos tracker-watch
just so that we can *feel* echo, *feel* witness, feel as if, well –

P is reappearing *in remembrance of you*.
As if Phanta by a different name
called up the landline for connection.

I think her words would taste much better
if I sliced them open. I think unpacking *Phanta*
    is like: *poem, poem, poem, porn.*

SONG WITH MUSCLE MILK

Take this cryptic correspondence as – a sound bite skirts my wonder.
Am I to crawl from out the bed to wonder – anti-wonder ?
The same time each day is just a concrete form of living, held
        in abstract.
Something *other* lies besides me – a lump of mask-strapped meat.
It is the breath through rubber tubes that lulls me back to sleep.
10am is sometimes noon, then ancient garbage piled up against
        the walls we wake to.
I care far too much for what the paint is called – name
        our future with emotions that I've slapped
        on lipless door frames.

Sylvie calls again to say – the home is dripping.
Chandler calls to say – *oh, so now you date a real man.*
I still like to put my headphones in with nothing
        playing; pretend it only takes one bulbous imperfection
        to make the whole thing beautiful.

Then I toss the tiny plastic bag back onto his cyborg meat-suit.
We fake our artificial sleep with four brand-new machines:
        first, the one that cleans the air – and then
        the one that moves it. The one that wets it – and the one
        that amplifies its depth through long experimental roars.

Maniac birds make chirp all night; they came here
        straight from hell.
The fifth machine drinks muscle milk, and is
        composed of human.

IV — AN INVITATION

_ ^ _

My sister and I are getting married.
Dear miser, miser – we are getting married !

All the clothes we stole become our dowry.
A registry made of mother's plastic jewels.
We will make hors d'oeuvres for you, and then transform into
a different family. We think we are people we think we are
phantoms *we think we are Kardashians*.

Our father's tongue rolls out his mouth.
It forms an aisle through the crowd.

Then we walk each other down into that earth baba – *silly baba* –
while everybody cheers and daddy, laughing, drowns.

We vow to keep it cute inside this castle til the end.

In the end, our future flies itself backwards into history
just like another angel, perfect slut.

_ ^ _

I will wed you to a hole, she says.
My very own *Mrs. Mean and Nasty*.
I will always clog the sink up with
your canned-tomato hair.

The dog swims in the pool all night;
the cat runs through the walls.
Mom crawls into her cage and sings
a bat tune. We are shocked
to hear the love implied by such
a wretched song.

We sing *caw caw caw* and chase the crows
Just so we can pet and bite them later in the yard.

We bury our umbilical cords and live happily ever after.
We dig up our umbilical cords, and live happily ever after.

POEM: EMPTY HOLE

My new desperation
is the holographic non-place
of a different woman's rage.
An empty hole that I kept filling up
with mattresses and rot.

The blood oxidized inside me long before
it trickled out. It was another empty hole
that you kept digging at the table.

You have a hoarse voice in your dream.
You find a plastic shovel we can lie in.
A shovel made for two.

And then, as if sleep were nothing more
than long patience for new hunger,
I wrote down ten new ideas every morning for three days.

_ ^ _

An empty hole cannot be seen, you say.
It's something, more like... *felt.*

But I'm sixty years old and still searching through
the groom's pockets for drugs.
One half of my jaw – with all its teeth – falls out.
I'm forty years old and fighting pity like disease.
It's always there. It's coming back.
Your empty hole is the disease.

Meanwhile, everyone else is *washing baby*
in the sink. Everyone *else* is dragging unkept promises
through the impending tornado, apocalyptic heat.
Everyone else is churning endless cloud-copy,
new candy, another chorus of *my snappy voice*
with its face pressed up against the wall.

_ ^ _

6am to not wake up. 7am to not meditate.
8am to not pick up the phone.
9am to not catch new men and
10am to not evolve them into *husband.*
11am to not unpack your bags
(like night) onto the floor.

For every beautiful woman, there's a boring dude
who hates to fuck her. Who said that ?
How my mother used to crawl around the room
to find discarded scraps of pill.

Paste the test results on fridge door.
Seal every number with an eyeball.
Wake me every hour on the hour.
Dig a hole with nothing bleeding, nothing torn.

THE WEDDING

The guests want to know how this story ends.
They use the ceremony to cycle between their open tabs:
    eyelash tints, incest porn, how to become more or less
    fatally infectious in the world.
The groom turns to the crowd and says – *what's the fucking point* ?
Nobody wants the experience. They just want the memories.
And this is starting to sound like a bad story.
Is this a bad story ?

We all look up from the party.
The answer is traced by an ugly plane, in the ugly sky.
As for the cake; the bridesmaids chose paper. One damp pile
of spaghetti topped with frozen whipped cream.
We made t-shirts with a picture of the bride's new toilet seat.
A photobooth that serves its own lemonade soup.

_ ^ _

After that, just some simple quotes
about finding love past the start-up.
Then some sharp-breasted mummies
getting muddy on a hill.

The groom grabs my hip in the stall; he grabs
through it. I am forced to speak fluent Latin
in order to get out. Then I build a broken ship.
The ship's for me; I am responsible.

When I cry, the bride places her hand
on my bloated stomach.
She explains that my screaming
is just another form of joyful singing.

The guests are starving in their dirty bathrooms
by the morning. The groom forgets to kill me in the end.

A BIRTHDAY SONG

How should I interrogate this desire to escape.
I think about the horses, how they might be mistaken
for camels. How I might be mistaken for anything at all.

Through the window, someone I love watches
an old woman pull a new dick from the sky.
Is wisdom like a battery ? More like Prius.

Sad ! I was sixty years old and still searching through high school
for sex. I was a reporter on campus I was looking for drugs.

Please list the events in your life in order to confirm.
Please take this class slow. List the good and the bad (please
don't worry about following this prompt correctly).

If you have any undealt-with trauma, please don't do
this exercise. Download the podcasts and stare at a pillow.
Just thirty minutes a day on every dread cycle should work.

RENOVATION SONG

I ask for total transformation and receive a vacuum-packed museum what the fuck.
These new shelves shoot like war ships out the walls into my mouth.
These hoes aren't loyal. We hide the guard, but seek the cat.
Every day I carry back and forth this mutant plant, wipe my tears
              on broken leaves that heave against an artificial sun.

I haunt the space before I enter – I haunt *through* it.
Turns out there is no present tense and never was.
These days I fill an absence with a candle. I carry
              the word CARE around, as if I have the right to.
              I dump CARE out the window. I toss CARE
              down the stairs. I watch CARE heaving on the floor.

On a longer shelf, one heavy bear that isn't quite a bear. In another bed, a man
              that isn't quite a man.
The trash – because I always must discuss the trash – it sucks our hunger dry.
Offensive shoes spread out the room and then they multiply.
The trash – it also multiplies.

Yeah, I said it. From all my dreams I wake up barren.
Turns out there is no actual creation.

Or, since I haven't said a single word for months, let me just begin
              with this: Dear Mom —

V — THE WOMEN HAUNT THEMSELVES

_ ^ _

A sound takes flight, and the brunch crowd starts their roaring. It's nothing new.
The new bitch licks her whore-lips through the broken quaran-clock. I fill my own
mouth with ten thousand marbles – cold machines (on the move) (in the dark).
I become the itchy meat-suit that you see here – these days – quite barren.
My reflection all stuffed up with hot boy-bots.

Meanwhile, I'd prefer to attach these good girls to my body.
Build a rat-nest full of language – write these garbage texts all night.

I ask them to say some words into my cellphone: "mini van," "heavy metal,"
"shopping bag," "hand lotion." I don't have a plan.
They would prefer to be married with their thin, tormented sisters.

The new bitch sends me bibles – broken mouse traps – empty code.
Then she sends a ghost – who eats up all our former kisses.

Eventually, this whole yard will be littered with my hairs – my pills – my bones.
And it is only the children who, rotting inside me, will still sit still to paint those bones.

CHANDLER'S SONG

O really who are you ?
I'm Chand —

those Chandler eyes tho bro.
How can we scuba D a force to make her
scuba O ?

I am Chand and not adored.

What she may, she might not know.

I tick tick when I think how quick
to make them quit of me.
I do it badly — do again
the same they want to see —
they want to see my pill my pill
my pill that melt my hand — I chant, I chant —

those Chandler eyes tho bro

DEAR CHAND

This prophecy is about you.
It takes a form
and uses it to build another in your chest.

The land in question is still a stranger
a string of shattered family attempts –

yes. A name cannot tell you what something is
and yet it still connects us in a web
of organized chants:

    Have you met the neighbors.
    They have a Chandler daughter.
    They have a   *char !*
                   Char !
                   Charmander !

Chand for just three minutes of watching her, herself –

DEAR CHAND

The set of ancient eyes she used for spying on herself
have been blended in and blotted out, her face
all fully fucked. With syllables, that is, that were never
fully formed.

Words that cannot travel mouth, the endless child seen
and smelling candies, singing to the car-pool, in a voice
of rain and sand.

Of this and that she's none. A mouth is a pushed-into
parti-colored crown; a cage over the throat
that connects into the head. Which connects
into the arms, into the holes between her legs.

In this hot lava of imagined worlds – they enjoyed
her smile. She forgot even their faces
which were somehow not the same.

AND WHEN IT RAINED

– the dog began to see a different dog.
A tiny slice of new fur danced in our TV.
But it was her. Dead weight for a good-girl is like –
oh yes – that's my girl ! – Or is it ?

Hello Sara, is that you ? Hi boo-boose.
Tonight will be a clammy cream with fish eggs thrown on top.
Grinch Spinach and a fat-free Turkish Yogurt Soup.
One small breast becomes a new dip for the table.
All movies are disgusting, did you know ?

I am getting up for bed, for they will not respect my genius.
I know that time is made of entropy or whatever, the reverse.
I know the molecules of family might regather
and become themselves inside a different corner
of the ceiling. Gravity is lies.

_ ^ _

If we move the paws of doggie
then what will happen to the rays of sun in California ?

The yolk drips down from mouth to mouth.
And now her credit sequence runs:
 yam intestines, hungry nipples, saliva
 nesting, noodle ghost.

What they refuse to understand is that –
none of this is information.
No, that is simply not
what *information* means.

Attic mom with canned tomatoes
and a set of baby teeth.

The puppy will become herself again
behind the ruins.

DREAM WITH CATS AND DOG

The dog is stiff. I am responsible. The cat is now a girl.
I'm trying to find the root of the little hair that sits at the back
of my throat. The villain has always been home.
Instead of "throat," I want to say "troat."
I am meant to babysit her.

Instead of babysitting, I'm obsessed with what this villain doesn't know.
Instead of babysitting, I'm shooting beams of salt over my shoulder.
May your journey flow like water. *Su gibi git gel.*

Still, I know I must confront this man
with something like a body.
I know the cats are singing monster slang (like bugs)
behind the walls.

As I said, it was winter. It was the return of the Sultan Saraoh.
The dog is stiff. I am responsible. The villain has always been home.

PAIN IS TELE

I just called to say that I am writing an elliptical piece about that
  telepathic injury. He who crawls out from the grave – *I mean,*
he has to know. We discuss the word *reverb* two times – decide it's part of
one-past-1am *I mean* – my residual obsession. Un-exorcize ? Un-able.
Thanks for listening. No – thank *you*. Not a lightbulb but the image
of a bulb in which I *too* believe
  goes off. Pain is *tele*. Pain is like – *you hurt me* – quote-end-quote.
Where quote is grave, but also all the desperate hands that dig it.

Happy belated. Wait for it – wait for it – as freezing persons rip apart
and melt the snow. She who did not catch the reference is – *survive*
– survive. *Quote-end-quote.* As we survive exhausting life inside the domes
of those that cast the longest stretch of distant past against us.

I was fundamentally prepared to *not* enjoy the day. Like Jesus himself –
I say to Sylvie, on the phone – I'll neither make nor clean my stain.

VI — THE DARK
CONTINUED DARK

_ ^ _

And then.

I was already in the habit.

I had still hopes.

I worked on her.

I weeped against the grid.

Nothing else came out.

I worked on him.

I was the martyr of my own timid implosions.

I said

    This is the history

        of zero-point history.

She said

    If you ever think to echo this voice –

don't.

A LETTER

The panic is_____ _____we have agreed.
The panic is_____we can't imagine.
The panic is_____we want but want_____
my father says_____is an_____American
___obsession____fuck a dove___has made a nest on
the fire_____escape_____escape___

The man has seen the nest.
He says he thinks of me.
He says that then again –
he does *not* think of me.
He says he simply cannot
be that dove.
I try to say that seeing is enough.

But what I really mean is:

I ENTERED THE DOOR

Wow. First let me ponder a yard. A yard can be a very quirky place,
much like a woman, damp old house. It is already December –
and this fictional version of my voice is starting to feel
quite neighborly. As if I would come to your memorial service
dressed up like a dragon ! – Ha ! – No, but let me explain
this story some more. So the photo of the cat-like dragon
is also a door. And the door is a sort-of… symbolism door.
Probably a dick, but possibly a doggie.

Remember when Tony Slightly Sketchy Wild Energy Wind Guy
noted the impeccable way that I was building his crypt into the side
of a hill ? The gifts of the crypt were often wonderful – but they were
also a burden. And isn't it adorable – to get this spooky enticement
from the old doctor's world ? I will let you know.
As StandupCoyote encourages: *"Woof*Woof*Wanna*Play?!"*

I ENTERED FANTASY

The hidden figure in the carpet
is always looking at that pussy
in the psychoanalyst's office.

The ice cube was a single hair
the better by which to freeze my rotting
eggs right into. Isn't that romantic ?

I'm sorry, do you know me ?
I have lived for sixty minutes, maybe even years.
Meanwhile, this man can turn facts about your *phanta*
straight up into gold.

    My students say *a body is an event.*
    They say their body *is* event.
    And then I love them, whoops –
    And then I love, then whoops –

_ ^ _

Meanwhile, there's a phantom daughter spinning through
the Boris Johnson in him. There's a blanket-type appearing
in his boy-o-boy façade.

> Whereas you ? You are not from here.
> You are trying to connect into
> that disconnecting triangle.

But that's just science, baby. History, some oracle shit.
That's just Phanta – and don't you wanna ?

> *Yes yes I do, the ghost.*

I'm sorry I don't care about like, any famous people.

It's not that I'm forbidden by any false song of obsession.
It's not even the old myth of a split tongue at my birth.

It's just that I care about something more – *how do you say*
(mmm snickers) – points out *Sylvie* in the crowd.

PHANTA'S HOUSE

Phanta meets Sylvie. Sylvie greets Chandler.
Chandler beats Phanta with a fine-toothed comb.

Sylvie at noon thinks that Chandler is ill.
She roams through the hall.
Chandler drinks Phanta and Phanta eats
Sylvie and Sylvie wants Phanta for Phanta
      needs pills.

Dash was our husband, although sadly, he got so mad
at himself for being fictional, that he stuck a harpoon gun in
his chest. Then he (hubbie) died. The good news is that
all eleven children had already climbed out of our mouths
by that time. The youngest was named Sara, Saray, or Saraoh;
she had diarrhea for almost all of 1995.

We are busy training roaches to grow ghost doves in their wombs.

VII – THE DIM
FLORESCENT LIGHT

— ^ —

All models off duty say: *Phanta number five*.
For something different, say: *these walls have glittered*

into fashion. Say we semi-hatched our egg-souls.
Say we named her forest grays.

Him spinning.
Him spinning. The world that still is the case.

Gimme that cold, that old florescent light.
Those ornaments. Gimme that dawn.

And as such, give to her
our mis-shreddings: white angels
fallen to that pond. The lock on this sandbox
is rusting: the only principle of our escape.

This carnival ends in a prison.
The world that is still, is the case.

PHANTA NUMBER FIVE

Ever since the bugs arrived inside my life (it doesn't matter).
Phanta let them in, as I have tried to write about:

     A dissertation on these new forms of (slip slap) white apology.
     A dissertation on these plagiarisms: what they are, and who they serve.
     A dissertation on the poetics of educational space: heat, lights, basements, trailers.
     A dissertation on the emails that simply lie and lie and lie.
     A *healthy* dissertation on unhealthy forms of intimacy.
     A dissertation on (slip slap) garbage texts, or my obsession with the ex.
     A dissertation on –

this fantasy SkyMall item that flowed from womb to womb to
     (slip slap) *Phanta* decked in light.

They always send me someone who they think is someone other.

They always come to name my body –
     name it *Phanta* – in the end –

_ ^ _

In the end – she will deflect
as if to plead her own defense:

> *My tonsil is a tadpole*
> *come from Balkans*
> *wrapped in shadow.*

My answer to the question
    is just your question out of tune.

And there are always two essay titles.
There are always two novels:

> The one in which she gets into the car
>   and fucks the guy, his empty code.

> The one in which
>   she takes the bus back home
>   and doesn't –

PHANTA'S SONG

How should I justify this practice ? I could say that it was never about accumulation –
the more you have, the more you get – but I didn't accumulate anything – so perhaps
I gave it all away ? I was offered precious content, and I made it disappear. So much
for translation – for transmission – *so much for transformation* – but at least I didn't
spend it – I could say. At least I simply let it rot into the distance. At least I danced
with the figure of a mushroom (mushroom-headed figure, the queen of all
the mushrooms, who does the mushroom dance).

Whoever rises into power should be forced to wear a bag over their heads.
Who said that ? Again I sat up crumpled on the couch. I pretended to have answers
to the questions on the codependency quiz – *as a coordinated form of entropy* – which is
the natural state (I think) of all our stupid lives – *in love* – I acted via text
as if I knew just how to read it. Thirty years of skipping past the part in books
with all the dates and names. Savage and salvage are newborn twins; perhaps
they profit. Perhaps they can untie these knots.

A CLOSET DISJUNCTION

My sister calls me on the blender; it was
our wedding gift. I tell her to avoid the burning
finger-touch of men. Next we write a *wikiHow*
to hate them for their touching. Next we're sitting
in the bedroom closet, with no more parrot, no more
blender, no more yelling, no more dove.

I can hear my own obsessions giggle in
the darkened corner. My sister is an infant, so I
transcribe her words. Then I try to sell them
like a book, I am a book; I am
responsible. These are my deepest praises
for an empire we *still* believe we own.

Like a villain, I pray these words will hide us in
(abyss abyss) then fling me up the stars —

HYPERPHANTASIA

Someone builds their own breath off the wind. Ready to wander – to breathe again
without a structure, or as a way to fast-escape this structure; anti-structure.
The truth is: I knew the sound before I used it up. *All song-like infestation in this nest.*

Will this story be about the roaches, in the end ? Overgrowth
gone understory, transcriptions without the politics of scribes.

But I wanted the material, the not-me, the rhyme in-anti-rhyme.
And I must be careful when I try to originate these ideas
with someone more specific.

If only P would tire of this dust and shit debris !
Because it's true: I love an empty code. But I don't like to have to force
the wrong notes out. And I don't know what to say about desire, or want –
        how it is mine, in the wanting, how it is not mine, in the wanting, how
        it's this wonky balance, baby
                        practice, how it's rot.

REFERENCES & NOTES

11 – "One, two, three, began" – After my mother, Alison Akant, always.
– "And what will you do with your one wild, precious life?"– After Mary Oliver's poem, "The Summer Day," *House of Light* (1990). ("Tell me, what is it you plan to do with your one wild and precious life?").

15 – "Hello, I'm Phanta, your personal expert on style." – After my sister's robotic friend Alexa, a Mattel Diva Starz doll, circa 2001. ("Hello, I'm Alexa…").
– "Phanta in the morning, Phanta in the evening, Phanta at suppertime" – After the advertisement for Bagel Bites, circa 1995. ("Pizza in the morning, Pizza in the evening...").

19 – "Jelly" – Poem after Kathy Acker's *Great Expectations* (1982).

21 – "The parrot my therapist keeps locked up in her office closet" – After my sister, circa 2017.

27 – "The Desire for an Entry" – Dedicated to the poet Meena Alexander (b. 1951 – d. 2018) and draws on language Meena spoke to me in her apartment, circa 2017.
– "This one is for the discipline of your soul" – After my waiter's description of a sherbet drink he served me in Konya, Turkey, after learning I'm unmarried, circa 2019.
– "With my own eight eyes" – After a song lyric by Ayla Çelik in "Bağdat" (2016). ("Bağdatı iki gözüm kapalı bulabilirimı iki gözüm kapalı bulabilirim, or "I can find Baghdad with my two eyes closed.")
– "I'll keep my mouth and my legs shut" – After my mother, on the phone with my sister, circa 2015.

28 – "His name is Dash, he hides a tree" – After my sister's imaginary husband, Dash, circa 1998.

29 – "Of the spinning girl, I should say" – After my mother's response to an email sent by my father, circa 2010.
– "I myself have been spying on myself" – After Alex Walton, circa 2012.
– "A grouse! A grouse! A personal grouse!" – After my grandmother, Virginia Heiserman, speaking to my sister, circa 2005.

34 – "The story of the thirsty cat" – After Elizabeth Yng-Wong's description of Van Gogh, circa 2020.
– "Beer, icky, ooch, dirt" – My own phonetic counting in Turkish: "one, two, three, four…"

35 – "The heap is eclipsed from the sentence" – After Sianne Ngai's *Ugly Feelings* (2005).
– "I arrived on top of you" – My own translation of the Turkish phrase "üstüme gelme," which roughly means "do not arrive on top of me," or "don't irritate me."
– "I also split in two. I visited both places." – Boris Groys and Andro Wekua's *Wait to Wait* (2009).

39 – "On the fourth day of the first day of the end" – After Shane McCrae's poem "Imagine the Day," posted on Twitter on November 6, 2020. ("On the fourth day of the first day of the end / I wake in blue, in gray that must be blue.")

41 – "I only notice when other people are ugly… not you" – After Yale Yng-Wong, circa 2020.

44 – "The home is dripping" – After Daisy Atterbury, circa 2018.

48 – "Mrs. Mean and Nasty" – After my mother's nickname for me, circa 2000.

49 – "A shovel made for two" – After a dream of Yale Yng-Wong's, circa 2020.

51 – "For every beautiful woman, there's a boring dude who hates to fuck her" – After Hala Alyan, circa 2021. But actually, who said that.

54 – "More like Prius" – After a text message exchange with Jessica Laser, circa 2020.

55 – "These hoes aren't loyal" – After song lyrics in Chris Brown's "Loyal," *X* (2014). "Let me just begin with this: Dear Mom" – After language in Kathy Acker's *Great Expectations* (1982).

61 – "They have a Chandler daughter" – After my father, describing the neighbors.

63 – "Grinch Spinach" – After my mother's text message to my sister, concerning dinner plans, circa 2014.

64 – "Yam intestines, hungry nipples, saliva nesting, noodle ghost" – After watching the ending of Juzo Itami's film, *Tampopo* (1985).

65 – "Su gibi git gel" – Invented Turlish phrase, roughly translates as: "Come and go like water."
– "With something like a body" – After Kathy Acker's *Great Expectations* (1982).
– "Monster slang" – After Gilles Deleuze's *A Thousand Plateaus* (1980).

66 – "Pain is Tele" – Poem dedicated to Jessica Laser on her birthday, May 29, 2020.
– "The reference" – After Emily Dickinson's poem "After great pain, a formal feeling comes" – (372) – (1830).
– "I will not clean my stain" – After a Reddit poster, circa 2020.

69 – "Zero-point history" – After the Turkish-to-English translation of a plaque at the E.U.-sponsored museum at the Göbeklitepe site in Eastern Anatolia, circa 2019.

71 – "I Entered the Door" – The quirky language that forms the backbone of this poem – as well as the original tagline *Woof*Woof*Wanna*Play?!* – has been lifted from visionary activist Caroline Casey – in a "re-mail" she sent to Yale Yng-Wong and Elizabeth Yng-Wong – on November 30, 2020. The email exchange was about a pair of stone Han Dynasty tomb doors, which were purchased by Yale's father Quing Yng-Wong from Hong Kong, circa 1995.

73 – "A blanket-type appearing" – After the Google translation of an advertisement for a blanket in the image of the Russian cartoon character Cheburashka on a Japanese wholesale website.
– "Boy-o-boy façade" – Boris Groys and Andro Wekua's *Wait to Wait* (2009).
– "Mmm snickers" – After Cher Horowitz, in *Clueless* (1995).

77 – "All models off duty say: Phanta number five" – After my mother, giving my brother a bath, circa 1995. ("A nudie on duty: policeman number five.")

78 – "They always send me someone who they think is someone other" – After language spoken to me by Meena Alexander, at a dinner, circa 2015.

80 – Poem after Anna Tsing's *The Mushroom at the End of the World: On the Possibility of Life in Capitalist Ruins* (2015).
– "Whoever rises into power should be forced to wear a bag over their heads" – After Yale Yng-Wong, circa 2021.

ACKNOWLEDGMENTS

Many thanks to the editors of the journals in which versions of these poems first appeared or are forthcoming:

"The Wedding" and parts of "A Birthday Song" were published in *160 Kilometres* in July 2021, for which they were translated into Turkish by Fatma Nur Türk. "Chandler's Song" and "Dear Chand" were published in *Gramma Press Daily*, October 2016. "Hyperphantasia" and "Song with Muscle Milk" are forthcoming in *Gulf Coast.*

Endless thanks and love to my family and friends, without whom none of the language, nor the sensibility, nor the writing of these poems would be possible: Adnan Akant, Alison Akant, Elizabeth Akant, Adam Akant, Rawaan Alkhatib, Ashley Colley, Katie Fowley, Jess Laser, Dan Poppick, Margaret Ross, Colby Somerville, Bridget Talone, Katie Taylor, and Elizabeth Yng-Wong.

To Daisy Atterbury, my constant caller.
To Caroline Casey, for working to "transmute unease into blessing."
To Adrienne Raphel and Hala Alyan, my writing witches and ha/bbs in psychic correspondence.
To Wayne Koestenbaum, for the exercises and energies.
To Meena Alexander, for the guiding voice and light.
To Yale Yng-Wong, for the original words, for the late-night editing, and for the fresh creative mind.

Thanks to the MacDowell Artists' Residency and to Willapa Bay AiR, for the support of time and space. Thanks to Cyndy Hayward and Jeff McMahon especially. Thanks to Stephanie Gicot for the time at Herdade do Pinheiro.

Thanks to my generous, careful, and attentive editors, Caryl Pagel, Daniel Khalastchi, and Alyssa Perry. Enormous thanks to the entire team at Rescue, working magic behind the scenes at every turn.
To Sevy Perez for the imaginative, impeccable, and always genius design.